BODY
MATH

PENNY DOWDY

mc **Marshall Cavendish**
Benchmark

New York

Library of Congress Cataloging-in-Publication Data
Dowdy, Penny.
Body math / by Penny Dowdy.
p. cm. -- (Math alive)
Includes bibliographical references and index.
ISBN 978-0-7614-3215-9
1. Mathematics--Juvenile literature. 2. Body, Human--Juvenile literature.
3. Human anatomy--Juvenile literature. 4.
Mathematics--Experiments--Juvenile literature. I. Title.
QA40.5.D69 2009
513--dc22

The photographs in this book are used by permission and
through the courtesy of:
Sebastian Kaulitzki/ Shutterstock: 4, 5 , Michael Braun Photography/
Istockphoto: 6-7, Yakobchuk Vasyl/Shutterstock: 8-9, Jonathan Larsen/
Shutterstock: 10-11, Digitalskillet/Shutterstock: 12, John Bailey/ Shutterstock: 13,
Vadim Kozlovsky/Shutterstock: 14, Ren   Mansi/Istockphoto: 16, PhotoCreate/
Shutterstock: 17, MarioPonta / Alamy: 18, Dragan Trifunovic/Shutterstock: 20,
Domen Colja/Shutterstock: 21, Craig McAteer/Shutterstock: 22, Catalin Plesa/
Shutterstock: 24, David Grossman/Photolibrary: 25, mandygodbehear/Bigstock:
26, It Stock RM/Photolibrary: 28-29,
Illustrations: Q2AMedia Art Bank

Cover Photo:Front: Kirsty Pargeter/Shutterstock; Julien Tromeur/ Shutterstock.
Back: UltraOrto, S.A/ Shutterstock
Half Title: It Stock RM/Photolibrary
Creative Director: Simmi Sikka
Series Editor: Jessica Cohn
Art Director: Sudakshina Basu
Designer: Prashant Kumar
Illustrators: Indranil Ganguly, Rishi Bhardwaj, Kusum Kala and Pooja Shukla
Photo research: Sejal Sehgal
Senior Project Manager: Ravneet Kaur
Project Manager: Shekhar Kapur

Printed in Malaysia
135642

Contents

The Body of Numbers

The human body is an interesting subject. Medical students spend years studying how all the different parts of the body work together. Artists paint, mold, and draw the human form, showing the body in movement—and at rest. Athletes train and strengthen their bodies, so they can compete and win at sports. The human body can even help a person better understand math!

Human Body Countdown

How does the body show math? Let's start with a countdown. Look at this list of small, simple numbers that have to do with the human body:

10: Humans have ten toes and ten fingers.

9: A woman usually carries a baby for nine months.

8: The **cranium**, or skull, encloses the brain. It is made up of eight bones.

7: Among the body's twelve pairs of ribs are seven pairs of "true ribs." Seven of the pairs connect to the sternum, the big bone running down the middle of the chest.

6: There are six different kinds of joints that can move in the human body. Joints are the spots where two bones come together.

5: There are five lobes, or spaces, in your lungs. The left lung has two, and the right lung has three!

4: The heart has four spaces, called **chambers**.

3: The stomach forms a new lining every three days. It needs a new lining that often because of all the acid in the stomach.

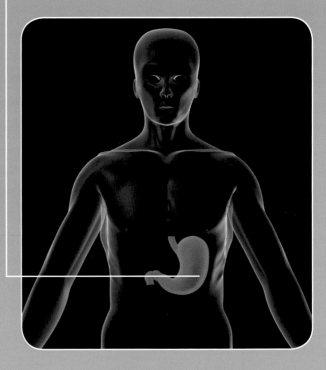

2: Humans have two lungs, two kidneys, two ears, two eyes, two legs, two feet, two arms, and two hands.

1: Each person has one head, one heart, one nose, and one liver.

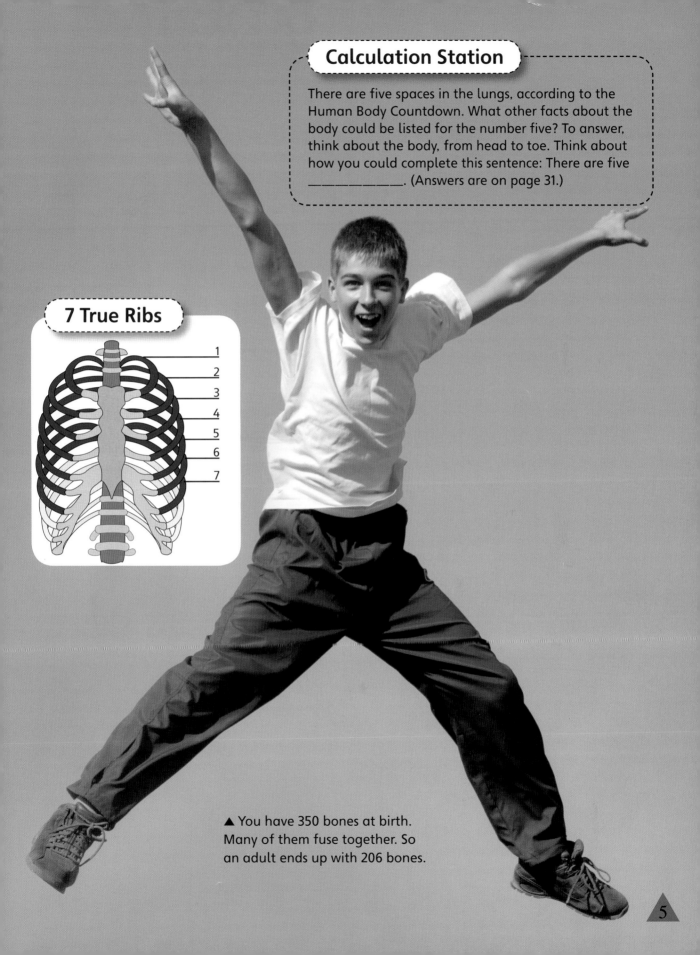

Calculation Station

There are five spaces in the lungs, according to the Human Body Countdown. What other facts about the body could be listed for the number five? To answer, think about the body, from head to toe. Think about how you could complete this sentence: There are five _____. (Answers are on page 31.)

7 True Ribs

1
2
3
4
5
6
7

▲ You have 350 bones at birth. Many of them fuse together. So an adult ends up with 206 bones.

Living Large

The human body has many large numbers on display, too. Did you know that there are about 100,000 hairs on the average person's head?

Each adult has about 10 trillion cells in his or her body. That number looks like this: 10,000,000,000,000. Think about that! Approximately 7 billion people live on Earth. That number looks like this: 7,000,000,000. If you do the math, it would take more than 1,400 planet Earths to hold as many people as one person has cells.

◀ The average person loses 60 to 100 hairs per day.

Hands-On Math: Skin Size

A grown male has about 2,790 square inches of skin. Let's figure out how much skin this is.

What You Will Need:
- 11" x 17" sheet of paper
- Calculator

What to Do:

1 Find the area of the paper, in square inches. (Multiply length times width.)

2 Divide 2,790 by the number you got in step 1. Round that answer to the nearest whole number.

Explain Away

The area of the sheet of paper is 187 square inches (11 times 17). If you divide the number of square inches of a grown male's skin by the square inches in a sheet of paper, you can "see" how many pieces of paper it would take to equal the amount of skin. (Answer is on page 31.)

The Small Stuff

Some numbers related to your body are really small. For example, your fingernails only grow about 0.004 (four-thousandths) of an inch each day. That is equal to 0.1 millimeter.

Have you ever had an earache? The pain seems to fill up your whole head. However, most earaches are caused by fluid or germs in a space that is only about 1-1/2 inches long.

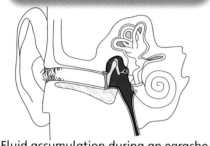

During an Earache

Fluid accumulation during an earache

Taste buds are even smaller. One taste bud is about 100 **microns** tall. It is only half as wide as that. So how big is a micron? A micron is 1/1,000,000 (one-millionth) of a meter, so a taste bud is about 0.0004 (four-ten-thousandths) of an inch tall. That's way too small to measure with a ruler.

Sizing Up a Taste Bud

0.0004

tenths
hundredths
ten-thousandths
thousandths

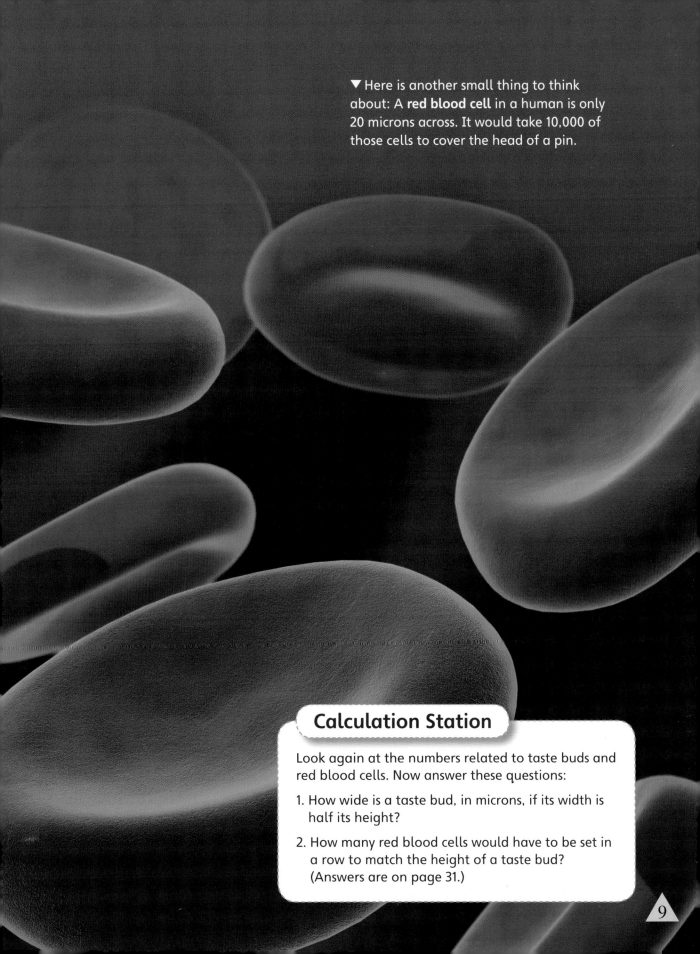

▼ Here is another small thing to think about: A **red blood cell** in a human is only 20 microns across. It would take 10,000 of those cells to cover the head of a pin.

Calculation Station

Look again at the numbers related to taste buds and red blood cells. Now answer these questions:

1. How wide is a taste bud, in microns, if its width is half its height?

2. How many red blood cells would have to be set in a row to match the height of a taste bud? (Answers are on page 31.)

The Need for Speed

The fastest runners in the world can run 100 yards—the length of a football field—in less than ten seconds. The best swimmers still take nearly one minute to swim the same 100 yards.

Most people are not among the fastest runners or swimmers inthe world, but all people can say they are fast at some things. A sneeze actually blows out of the nose at a speed of about 100 miles an hour. The body sends messages to your brain at a speed of 180 miles an hour.

The eyes move very quickly, too. The muscles in an eye move in 1/100th (one-hundredth) of a second. Compared to that, a blink is slow. It takes about 3/10ths (three-tenths) of a second to blink. Yet that's still so fast, it would be hard to measure without special tools. No wonder people talk about fast things as happening in "the blink of an eye."

▼ Record-setting sprinters can reach speeds of 27 miles (43.5 kilometers) per hour.

Hands-On Math: Sneeze Speed

The speed of the human sneeze gives you an idea of the power in our bodies. Some of the most powerful storms are hurricanes and tornadoes. Let's compare the speed of a sneeze with those of different storms.

What You Will Need:

Encyclopedias or online reference material, such as:

http://reference.aol.com

www.encyclopedia.com

education.yahoo.com

encarta.msn.com

What to Do:

1 Find the minimum speeds for Level 1 through Level 5 hurricanes.

2 Find the minimum speeds for Level 0 through Level 6 tornadoes.

3 List the speeds of a hurricane, a tornado, and a sneeze in order from slowest to fastest.

Explain Away

How would you explain the speed of a sneeze compared to hurricanes and tornadoes? (Answers are on page 31.)

11

What Are the Odds?

Many qualities make a person unique. Many of these qualities are determined by how **genes** from a child's parents combine in their child. Genes carry many of the **traits** that people have. A person may be born with brown, black, golden, or red hair, for instance, based on his or her genes.

Punnett Squares

A **Punnett square** is a tool used to show traits (for example, hair color) that parents have. This tool also shows how likely those traits are to be passed on to their children.

Let's look at eye color. Different genes are associated with different eye colors. Each person gets two genes for eye color, one gene from the mother and one gene from the father. One of those genes will dominate. In other words, only one eye color will show up in the child.

On a Punnett square, genes are shown with certain symbols, such as **B** for brown eyes and **b** for blue eyes. The brown eye color gene gets a big **B** because brown eye color is dominant. When a baby ends up with the gene pair **B b**, that baby is born with brown eyes.

In the Punnett square below, the father's two genes for eye color are **B b**. (He has brown eyes.) The mother has **b b**. (She has blue eyes.)

		Father	
		B	b
Mother	b⟶	B b	b b
	b⟶	B b	b b

The Punnett square is filled in going down and across, to show the possibilities. In this case (see the red combinations), there are two ways the parents' genes can combine to make brown eyes. There are two ways the genes can combine to make blue eyes. This baby would be equally likely to have either brown or blue eyes.

▲ Traits like eye color run in families.

Calculation Station

Make a Punnett square to show a father with B B brown eyes and a mother with **b b** blue eyes. What are the chances their baby would have blue eyes? (Answer is on page 31.)

13

Genes for Many Traits

Being able to stick a thumb backward more than 45 degrees is one kind of trait. Doing that is called hitchhiker's thumb. Having ear lobes that do not stick out is another one. In order for a person to have ear lobes that are attached to the head, the person would need two genes for attached ear lobes.

Let's use a Punnett square to see how this works. We can call the gene for attached ear lobes **a**. We can call the gene for detached ear lobes **D**. The capital letter shows that if you have one gene for each kind of earlobes, your earlobes will be **D**. They will be detached. Look at the squares to see how it works.

Look at all of the pairs. The odds are much more likely that a person has ear lobes that are not attached!

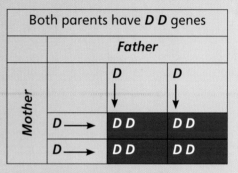

Both parents have D D genes

Mother		Father	
		D	D
D →	D D	D D
D →	D D	D D

Both parents have a D genes

Mother		Father	
		a	D
a →	a a	a D
D →	a D	D D

Father has a D, Mother has D D

Mother		Father	
		a	D
D →	a D	D D
D →	a D	D D

Father has D D, Mother has a D

Mother		Father	
		D	D
a →	a D	a D
D →	a D	D D

▼ People can have hitchhiker's thumb on one hand but not the other.

14

Here is a list of traits seen in people. Let's see which trait from each pair is more likely to show up.

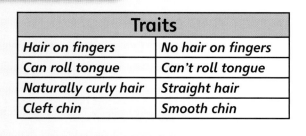

Traits	
Hair on fingers	No hair on fingers
Can roll tongue	Can't roll tongue
Naturally curly hair	Straight hair
Cleft chin	Smooth chin

What You Will Need:

- Paper
- Ten people
- Pencil

What to Do:

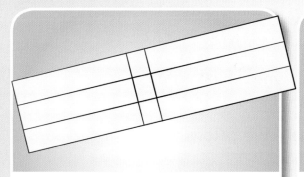

1 Make a table with two columns for each of the three pairs of opposing traits.

2 Ask ten people which of these traits they have. Place a mark in the appropriate column for each answer.

3 Based on your results, circle the trait from each pair that you believe is least likely to show up in people.

4 Check your results by doing research on genes and traits in encyclopedias and other reference sources.

Explain Away

Imagine if you had only asked one person. Why do you think is it better to ask ten people than one?
(Answer is on page 31.)

Blood Type

Hair color and eye color are determined by genes. The ability to fight a specific disease can be passed along from parents, too. Even something like blood type is determined by genes.

Basic Combinations

There are four basic blood types: A, B, AB, and O. Here is how they combine:

- If A combines with A or O, then the blood type is A.

- If B combines with B or O, then the blood type is B.

- If A and B combine, then the blood type is AB.

- The only way a person can have type O blood is to have two Os!

You would think that because A and B happens in two kinds of combinations, there would be more A or B blood types than O. Amazingly, you are more likely to find a person with type O blood than anyone else!

Look at the table below:

Blood Types in the United States	
Blood Type	Percent of People with the Blood Type
O	46%
A	39%
B	11%
AB	4%

▼ Almost 50 percent of people in the United States have type O blood.

▶ About 32,000 pints of donated blood are needed daily in U.S hospitals.

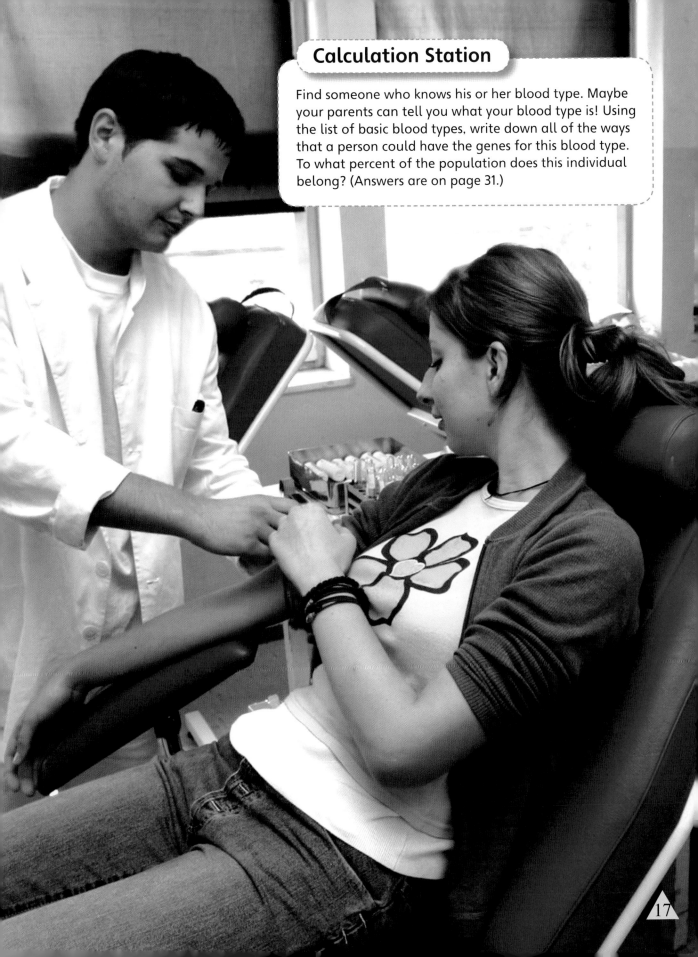

Calculation Station

Find someone who knows his or her blood type. Maybe your parents can tell you what your blood type is! Using the list of basic blood types, write down all of the ways that a person could have the genes for this blood type. To what percent of the population does this individual belong? (Answers are on page 31.)

Protection and Probability

We all value our bodies, but some people pay to protect their body parts. How? They buy insurance.

Piano players insure their fingers. Ballet dancers insure their legs. A famous singer, for instance, once bought $1 billion worth of insurance on her legs. Why? She was going to show her legs in an advertisement. If her legs were hurt before she did the work, she would not be able to earn the money for appearing in the ad.

The insurance was meant to pay for expenses if an accident were to happen to her legs. It was to help pay for the possible loss of income, too. Insurance companies look at the **probability**, or likelihood, of such accidents happening. They look at the **odds**. Then they figure out an amount to charge people for protection.

More people *pay* for insurance than ever use the insurance. Yet many people like knowing that there would be help if they needed it.

▲ The thumb, index finger, and middle finger are used most often in piano playing.

Hands-On Math: What Are the Odds?

Collect data to predict odds. It will not be as exact as the numbers insurance companies use. Yet it will point toward the kind of math these companies use to figure out how likely it is that something will happen.

What You Will Need:

- One pair of number cubes

What to Do:

1 Roll the pair of number cubes 50 times. Add the two numbers of the dots that are face up each time.

2 Make a list of the 50 totals you rolled.

3 Look at the list. Use the results to guess, or predict, how many times you would roll a 2 if you rolled the pair of number cubes 30 times.

4 Test your prediction by rolling the pair of number cubes 30 times.

Explain Away

Now think about which total of the two numbers has a higher probability, or shows up more often, than the others. Why? (Answers are on page 31.)

Perfectly Typical People

A **ratio** is a fixed relationship between two things. Mathematicians have developed a way to measure people's physical features and to show which measurements seem to please the most people.

The Perfect Man

A man named Vitruvius lived more than two thousand years ago. He wrote about how the perfect man would look. If the man stood with his arms stretched out, the measure would be the same as his height.

The arm spread and the height of the Vitruvian man are the same. This means the ratio of stretch to height is 1:1:

- The ratio of the width of his shoulders to his height is 1:4.

- The ratio of the distance from the top of his head to the middle of his chest to his height is 1:4.

- The ratio of the distance from the middle of his chest to the top of his leg to his height is 1:4.

- The ratio of the distance from the top of his leg to the bottom of his knee to his height is 1:4.

- The ratio of the distance from the bottom of his knee to the bottom of his foot to his height is also 1:4.

Although many people don't fit the Vitruvian model, most are surprisingly close!

Calculation Station

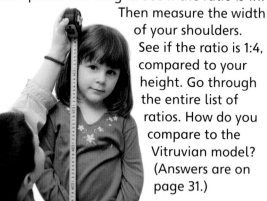

Take measurements of yourself, as described above. Use a measuring tape and keep track of the measurements on a piece of paper. A parent or partner can help you. Measure arm spread and height. See if the ratio is 1:1. Then measure the width of your shoulders. See if the ratio is 1:4, compared to your height. Go through the entire list of ratios. How do you compare to the Vitruvian model? (Answers are on page 31.)

▼ Leonardo da Vinci made a famous drawing, showing a man's body ratios inside a square and circle. We call such drawings Vitruvian man, after Vitrivius.

The Golden Ratio

One well-known ratio is the Golden Ratio, also called **phi** (pronounced FEYE). The Golden Ratio is found in art, plants, buildings—and even in people. Phi is about 8:5 (or 8 ÷ 5).

Think about paintings and buildings. If the ratio of height to width is 8:5, our eyes find it more pleasing than if what we are looking at is wider or taller than that. The ratio just looks "right." The pyramids in Egypt have a height to base ratio of 8:5, for example.

◄ This pyramid has four triangles for walls and a square for a base.

Hands-On Math: Right Ratios

The ratios between parts of the human body contain many examples of the Golden Ratio. Take some measurements and see how "golden" people can be.

What You Will Need:

- Measuring tape
- Calculator
- Paper
- Pencil

What to Do:

Make a table that looks like this one:

	Measurement A		Measurement B	A ÷ B
Elbow to wrist		Wrist to longest fingertip		
Shoulder to fingertip		Elbow to fingertip		
Height		Distance from navel to heel		
Height of ear		Width of ear		

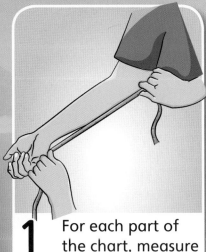

1 For each part of the chart, measure and record the lengths in inches.

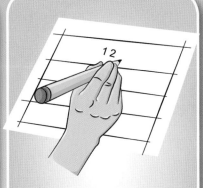

2 Circle the values in the left and right columns that are near the Golden Ratio.

3 Repeat steps 1 through 4 for a partner's measurements, if possible.

Explain Away:

When measuring in inches, you probably had to round off some of the numbers. If you like, you can try the exercise using centimeters. That can be more exact. (Answers are on page 31.)

Using Math in Art

Each of the following pairs is an example of the Golden Ratio in the human face. This means that the first measure divided by the second measure is near 1.618.

- The length of the face: the width of the face

- The length from the lips to where the eyebrows meet: the length of the nose

- The length of the face: the length from the tip of the chin to where the eyebrows meet

- The length of the mouth: the width of the nose

- The width of the nose: the distance between the nostrils

- The length between the pupils: the distance between the eyebrows

Remember that the Golden Ratio is about 8:5. When 8 is divided by 5, the answer is 1.618. This number is very close to 1.5.

You can use the ratios in your drawings, too. Let's say you are drawing a face that is 4 inches wide. To decide how long to make the face, look at the first pair of ratios in the list. Think about how you can make the length of the face match the Golden Ratio. The number 4 times 1.5 is 6. That means the length of the face should be about 6 inches.

Another way to think about it is this: the first measure roughly equals the second measure plus half the second measure. So the length of the face should be about 4 plus 2. (The second measure is 4, and half of 4 is 2.)

◀ The length of the mouth is compared to the width of the nose.

Calculation Station

Draw a face. Use the Golden Ratio, a ruler, and the measured pairs listed on page 24. (Answers are on page 31.)

Many Measures

Anthropometry is a word that means "studying the measurements of people." In the 1800s a French police officer started taking from people he arrested what he called eleven certain measurements. He found that the numbers were as unique as a fingerprint.

No two people would have the same eleven numbers—not even twins! The eleven measurements have been taken of many people over many years. They have been taken in many different countries. Everywhere you go, it seems, these measurements are indeed unique for each person. Each one of us is special.

Are you curious about the eleven measurements? They are shown in the table on the next page, in Hands-On Math.

▶ Perhaps the most important measurement is the wideness of your smile.

Hands-On Math: Uniquely You

Find your body measurement "fingerprint."

What You Will Need:
- Tape measure
- Paper
- Pencil
- Parent or partner

What to Do:
Make a chart like this one.

Measurement	You	Partner
Height		
Length from left shoulder to right middle finger when right arm is raised		
Length from head to tailbone, taken when seated		
Length from the top middle of head to top of the forehead		
Width of the forehead		
Length of right ear		
Length of left foot		
Length of left middle finger		
Length of left elbow to tip of middle finger		
Width of cheeks		
Length of left little finger		

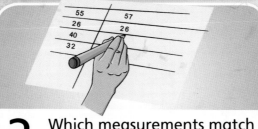

1 Record the eleven measurements you take.

3 Which measurements match for both of you?

2 Take the measurements of the person who helped you.

Explain Away:
Why can police use this information to identify people? (Answer is on page 31.)

Using Body Measures

The first use of anthropometry was to help stop criminals in their tracks. However, there are many reasons to measure people.

Think about people who make cars. They need to know the sizes of an average man and woman. This helps them make car seats that feel right to people who buy the vehicles. Imagine if the seats were too big or too small!

Clothing companies use measurements to set sizes for clothes. A company makes a size eight dress to fit a size eight person. A shoe company makes shoes and boots in special sizes. Many businesses must use anthropometry to be successful.

Scientists in space programs must understand anthropometry when they build space shuttles and space stations. They need to make sure the rooms are comfortable enough for astronauts. Body math is needed everywhere—even in space!

▶ Basketball sizes are determined by the average hand size of people in several age groups.

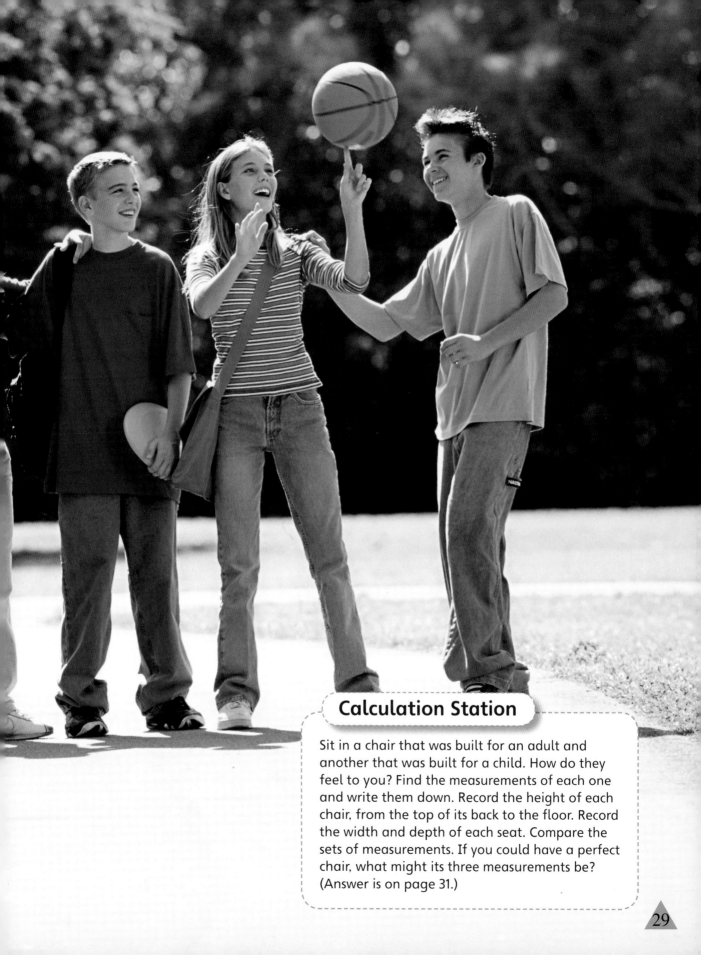

Calculation Station

Sit in a chair that was built for an adult and another that was built for a child. How do they feel to you? Find the measurements of each one and write them down. Record the height of each chair, from the top of its back to the floor. Record the width and depth of each seat. Compare the sets of measurements. If you could have a perfect chair, what might its three measurements be? (Answer is on page 31.)

Glossary

anthropometry The study of people's body measurements.

chamber An enclosed space.

cranium Part of the skull that protects the brain.

gene A code for passing qualities from parent to child.

micron Unit of measure that is one-millionth of a meter.

odds When one outcome is favored over another.

phi Number that represents the Golden Ratio (1.6180339887).

probability The chances that something might happen.

Punnett square Diagram used to show gene pairs.

ratio Relationship of quantity, amount, or size between two things.

red blood cell Cell that takes oxygen to tissue.

taste bud Part of the tongue that senses taste.

trait Distinguishing quality or inherited characteristic.

Answer Key
Calculation Station

p. 5: There are five fingers on each hand and five toes on each foot, five senses, the human skin weighs about five pounds, and there are five parts of the brain.

p. 9: 100 (microns) divided by 2 = 1. 50 microns 100 (microns) divided by 20 = 2. 5 red blood cells.

p. 13: There is no possibility that the baby will have blue eyes.

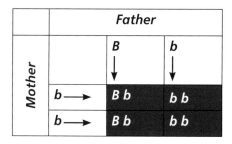

p. 17: Type A should list AA or AO. In the United States, 39% of people are this type.

Type B should list BB or BO. In the United States, 11% of people are this type.

Type AB should list AB. In the United States, 46% of people are this type.

Type O should list OO. In the United States, 4% of people are this type.

p. 20: Most people will be surprised at how close they match the ratio.

p. 25: Drawings should show the 1:1.5 ratio for each of the measurement pairs listed. So, for example, if the face is 5 inches wide, 5 times 1.5 is 7.5. So the face should be 7.5 inches tall.

p. 29: It is likely that a perfect chair would be somewhere between an adult's chair and a child's chair in dimensions. The answer should have a height for the chair back and a width and a length for the seat.

Hands-On Math

p. 7: The surface area of a man's skin is about 15 sheets of paper.

p. 11:
Hurricanes	Tornadoes
Level 1, 74.	Level 0, 40.
Level 2, 96.	Level 1, 73.
Level 3, 111.	Level 2, 113.
Level 4, 131.	Level 3, 158.
Level 5, 156.	Level 4, 208.
	Level 5, 261.
	Level 6, 319.

p. 15: More common: No hair on fingers. Can't roll tongue. Straight hair. Smooth chin. Less common: Hair on fingers. Can roll tongue. Curly hair. Cleft chin. With a larger group, predictions will be more accurate.

p. 19: There is a higher probability of rolling a 7 because there are more ways to get a 7 rolling two number cubes than any other number.

p. 23: The table should be complete, but the method of measurement is left to the person who answers. Tape measures often give both imperial and metric measures. For smaller body parts like the height and width of an ear, it can be easier to use centimeters, rather than fractions of an inch.

p. 27: Measurements will vary, but the entire table should be completed. Police could use the measures to identify someone without a driver's license or other means of identification.

Index